Free Verse Editions
Edited by Jon Thompson

Dear Reader

Bruce Bond

Parlor Press
Anderson, South Carolina
www.parlorpress.com

Parlor Press LLC, Anderson, South Carolina, 29621

© 2018 by Parlor Press
All rights reserved.
Printed in the United States of America
S A N: 2 5 4 - 8 8 7 9

Library of Congress Cataloging-in-Publication Data on File

978-1-60235-280-3 (paperback)
978-1-60235-281-0 (PDF)
978-1-60235-282-7 (Epub)

1 2 3 4 5

Cover design by David Blakesley.
Cover image: "Night Grove" by Aron Wiesenfeld. Used by
    permission.
Printed on acid-free paper.

Parlor Press, LLC is an independent publisher of scholarly and
trade titles in print and multimedia formats. This book is available
in paperback and ebook formats from Parlor Press on the World
Wide Web at http://www.parlorpress.com or through online and
brick-and-mortar bookstores. For submission information or to
find out about Parlor Press publications, write to Parlor Press,
3015 Brackenberry Drive, Anderson, South Carolina, 29621, or
email editor@parlorpress.com.

Contents

Contents

The end is unconscious as soon as it is reached.

—Emmanuel Levinas

Dear Reader

Dear Reader

1.

Dear shush of oceans, page after page, you
who make me feel more fortunate and small,

I too am setting out, my eye lit up
to the horizon with all that never arrives.

I eat my books with a hunger that rivals
the sadness of monsters in books. I am nowhere

without them: the beasts who never die.
They gnaw at me like oceans at the shore.

Dear ocean wave, I am reading your letter
the letter I am reading. The shore advances.

The shore retreats. Our breath is everywhere.
Perhaps I would be more full of monsters

if not for songs that make them bearable.
Or books that spill the blood they would conceal.

2.

To be one is odd, and one over one
still one, cold as the numbers ledgered

down the long column of last effects.
And it takes a little cold beauty to think

a violence reducible to what it means.
A knife as particular, it is silent, swift,

stubborn as the rock the philosopher kicks
in defiance of world as slumber and idea.

Cruelty has a face. It has the neighbor
window to mirror ours before we vanish.

But murder is schooled in years of evasion
of one's pain and the faces it lays bare.

It is cold as light the neighbor finds
shameless, sexless. A sharper way to read.

3.

About now the monsters grow more lovely
and why not. Why suffer the transfusion

of our blood into their bodies on high.
All the tension in the banter has come

to this, to the moment that draws the couple
closer with the violence of a new song.

About now the monsters walk among us
as dolls and children and the great night sky,

stars that pin our stories to the dark.
And if the star looks a little anguished

at the moment of union, it is not instinct
as the thoughtless know it, but one that tears

loose of thought, or blossoms into cries,
hearts leaping in one wilderness, like deer.

4.

When I was young, I knew there were ideas
that laid their faces on the face of night.

I felt the cataract of daylight falling
into privacies of sleep. One enormous

wilderness, so long as we are sleeping.
I knew this, as dream sometimes knows

it is dreaming, when the knowledge is not
dream alone. Some nights blur into one

night, one long rehearsal for retirement.
No doubt I want more choices at that hour,

in reveries more odd than liberated.
Dear Reader, I have not forsaken you,

the idea of you, for the rule of language
we break now like glow sticks in the dark.

5.

Together is darker than the word that takes
its place. To cast a shadow over the page

you read, over the body you lie against,
it makes understanding more personal,

in ways that instinct or the known alone
is not. Instinct that is water falling

into water. Or so we understand
when reflection calls the falling ours.

I chime a spoon of meat into a bowl
in the morning and my one cat makes

the sound of sneakers in the gym. Then
her sweet plea disappearing in the bowl.

Instinct that is the star consumed at dawn,
the pretext of our silence. More deep than long.

6.

The small death, it becomes us. It becomes,
in time, our great absorption into no thing.

You with your mouth, me with my echo *there,
there,* we are giving in to space between us.

The small death between lovers in a car
parked at the edge of shore, it empties them.

Death as the blossom drawn through the eye
of the vase, through the clear black glass.

It holds so little in its grasp, the zero
of the cathedral rose that holds us to it.

Why we call it ours is anyone's guess:
the death that names our life before a life.

My first word was a figure against a ground.
And in it: you. The hunted, wanted, feared.

7.

Somewhere the chime in the morning bowl
calls the animal to what it does not

understand. And yet it reads. It eats.
It hears the light of dawn break like bread.

Long ago, when my friend was gone,
I fed his cats. I watched them grow more

and more excited to see me in the morning.
Not me as some deep recess to explore,

the word-closet who thinks of them in closets.
But as emergent: the emergency color

of one of many blooms a bee might choose.
That hum of the swarm selects. It finds

the better fields of the many and turns
them into honey. Thus the language of bees.

8.

Thus these bees as readers in a library
of illuminated books. Not quite friends,

though as I read, the books I love feel
more as I feel, their pages worn dark

along the margins, their illustrations burned
in me, like roses in a patch of snow.

I give my face to them, to the color
they return to letters and all who write them.

Take this book of hours I am reading
as we speak, these winter scenes radiant

as midnight diners. When I close its cover,
I continue to hold a lantern in the dark

instinctual fire that melds: word to world,
heaven to earth. Sweet animal to bowl.

9.

I choose to remember days that choose me
in return. Take this hour, this gardener

in a book of prayers. Take the blue
of winter, figured against the lifeless ground.

Dear memory, who if not you invents
a language, deep in the bodies of others.

Who makes some sense of ours. The rain that falls
(though the hole of one particular sky)

it just might reach us long after storm.
It just might be a child of experience

that drizzles in shadows into pools of light.
No task at hand to change this. No summons

of collective praise or lack of praise.
No wound washed clean in the blood of seeing.

10.

The ghost-face of what we suffer lies
across the glass between us. Who am I

to strike my eye from the eye I strike,
to strike the words I feel ashamed of.

Stranger, have you been there all along.
Hard for me to imagine otherwise,

and still have things I need to discuss.
Ink dries. Then it welters in the eye.

Lamplight needles and threads the pearls of rain.
At least this is the hope. The lantern held

by the dark incisions of ink on white.
Always more, says the skeptic hope.

Like despair that way. The desire
that learns it cannot, must not, be desired.

11.

Always more, say the afterlives of two
in the dark. Always more, the smoke

they blow through a quietude of words.
And in the dome above them, the stars

that care for no one. It makes them sharp
as jewels, their lives small and fortunate.

Not that desire needs to die to make it
light. But there is always more around it.

More, says the boy at meditation
whose prospect of arrival must be hopeless.

More, my friend once said to himself
and so he drowned himself in wine. His body

an empty bottle he emptied bottles into.
As if to complete the circle. And close.

12.

More, says the character who transfers
stones from pocket to pocket, finding

comfort in the recursive machinery
of progress. More, says the artificial

friend who, in death, is more of the same.
Just listen to the clock at the far end

of the conference table. The broken hand
inside that twitches, audibly, in place.

Numbers alone are literal, it says,
alone in the dull pastorals of phonebooks.

All we like sheep. Numbers alone.
Sweet autistics of the sign kingdom.

They play a music with no music in it.
Only a description, an effigy, a stone.

13.

We find our place on maps. We signature
our stones in the language of restraint.

And still the numbers alone are what they are.
Leave it to gospels to redden into wine.

But they are not wine. They are the glass
we drain to feed us. The words are listening.

Whose glass is this anyway. Whose voice.
Whose congress drawn through the congress

of the *the* regime. There is no safe place.
No map there to get us there. Abstention

too files a claim, however summoned
to shop in times of crisis. With every word,

I cast my vote. With every mention of rain,
the memory of rain. The silent pavement.

14.

I followed my breath so I might find it
outside the thought of one breath or another.

To breathe is to breathe through a face unseen
as others see it. I followed my thoughts

to a pause in the dialogue of breathing.
The trees of nerves are beautiful in winter.

Sometimes I do it in a group, with one
or two, who never are so friendly. After.

Not mean. Just solitary trees in winter.
However inside or outside the difference

of thought, they, as them, are nowhere near.
Call them the space around the thought. Or space

around the space, which in turn says nothing.
Across the otherwise congregate silence.

15.

The call of freedoms other than our own.
They make a language by human instinct

other than one's own alone. We all suffer
the same illusions now, or so I imagine.

Those of us who meditate together,
we all watch our solitude get longer,

more bearable, more negotiable. A part.
This is not to say you have escaped.

Besides. What is there to escape.
Something your father said that hurt you,

it is in there, inside the missing father.
Books of dreams crackle into flame,

and just watching makes it all feel less
unnerving. You here, fire there. Alive.

16.

Then I followed my breath to a place of rest.
In the air a vague wind, an idea of rest.

Truth is, I am always in two places.
I am always the writer who reads and finds

something missing. When I close my eyes,
I see the friend who drank himself blind.

I read to him. Which comes easily.
Too easily given the difficult things I say.

Sometimes when a dream breaks, I sleep
a little more. The elms outside take on

the light I give them. But it is not my gift.
Not mine alone, they wear the accent

of gifts that need a scarcity about them.
Like lilies in the darkness of the pond.

17.

You can wander the sexual streets of London
to where they lead, if you are patient.

And here you are, among the canvases
of the free museums, the rivers of instinct

disciplined, held, released in the lilies.
Walls rise flooded in the petals and vines.

Such holding gives back a better version
of magnanimity and animal hunger.

This monster of light, this reaching for it,
it says something beyond the blue movies

whose unions end in too many questions.
Or too few. It says there is language

in the wilderness that sweetens the air
it breathes and gives us. Long ago, in stillness.

18.

Say we speak a tongue we do not know,
our nets thrown deep beyond the object,

past the rot and minnows of the water,
the sizzle of the mayflies, the s in yes.

Say our instinct flowers into embrace,
sunk, face-down, against the April water.

It just might loosen the noose of the collar,
the burden of the language left unspoken.

Even dreams give us choices to make
into the ways we read them. It is in there:

the afternoon a painter so loved the pond
he placed a canvas in the way. So loved

the eye-black water bled through the iris.
So he might step away, with us. And see.

19.

I follow my breath to a small museum
of small objects I squint my eyes to read.

I have a will in me I barely know.
As if desire has choices to make without me.

So, as I stand above the tiny house
where I once lived, I talk. I confess.

The way loneliness does to a stranger
or a cat. Do not touch, says the museum

guard to a child. And the door of the house
squeaks on its hinges. Do not breathe,

says the violins of flies above the lilies
and things so small you cannot reach them.

And so I watch the child. How he touches
his face. And without thinking, I touch my own.

20.

Long ago I drank the grape juice and prayed,
bound by word to wine, by wine to blood,

blood to the blood of others, the common
flesh, our savior, too large or small to see.

I drank from the paper cup I crumpled
with *amen,* because there was a god

in wine's encouragement. It made me small.
For I was a long way from witnessing

the more inclusive picture no one does
in one thing. Take death. Or one such death.

One bird in the gutter on Wabash Street.
It said nothing to me. And again it said,

Isn't it odd, being alive like this,
a child inside the largest day of the year.

21.

The choir of the flock would be nothing
without the path of voices that began

in terror and desire, fighting to breathe.
Each bird among the others is possessed

by a spirit of numbers that has no body.
A circle without center. Bird after bird.

Our Father, I once said in a great space
that gave back the resonance of walls,

wells. Every child here a choir of one.
My particular father was many to me.

He slapped me once, thinking I did
a thing I did not. If he felt bad later,

I do not know. Or know the many birds
my fathers scattered as I looked away.

22.

When a god hits earth, the world turns
into one small thing in the greater picture.

The father, a man, they are many men
inside of each. So people turn to gods.

Our Father, forgive us, I said, with him.
And wine blazed a path to the blood.

It labored to absolve our bodies of fear
and live. So yes. I was a little monster,

petty with greed, eager to leave home,
to walk the unfamiliar wilderness.

Some birds spill more blood, having flown.
A child of the child I was, I deserved

a slap for something, surely. Me.
Proud and small inside the spinning stars.

23.

To be one of the many night skies then,
the kind that navigates sailors in trouble

or lies down in the grids of cities I love,
I wanted nothing more. The whole picture

a circuit of streets, laws, the emptiness between.
The deep that is the shadow of the father

who bears a boy's sleeping body to bed.
Say what you will about our myth of myths

and the inner life, the small dark chamber
of ideas. I love the word *Idein*, to see.

I love to see, in one of the many skies,
the notion of one returning with his child,

how he breaks into small and smaller versions
of one, and why it is I need to see him.

24.

We choose our idols and words like friends
whose trust is free to turn against us.

Our choices come back as what one is,
one has, and is not yet. Like a broken

promise. Or the fire that takes a ghetto
to blaze its path into the lens. Cities

lit up with inner life, one part choice,
another fire. Such was the black and white

TV violence I watched when I was small.
My suffering got a little smaller that day,

my sentences shorter, the thought of inner lives
so enormous I could barely see them.

A stranger's slap comes for something he sees.
For some deep reason. Unspoken or unheard.

25.

Such was the burden of my unknown fortune.
My vague unspoken privilege like a TV

looted from the storefront and seen again
on my TV. I live by the power of choice

inside a power denied, the quiet violence
of money changing hands. The inner life

was everywhere. And everywhere a ghost.
Like gods or cities taken whole. And you,

Dear Reader, I can almost imagine you
as anyone now, though surely you are not.

You who are more particular than known.
And not just you, but the city you live in,

the street where I never met you, where words
cross a table between strangers. Like bread.

26.

Is it possible to talk alone with God.
I asked a particular god that once.

I talked a lot in silence when I was small.
And although I heard, I did not answer.

I do not know if I was mesmerized
or scared or content to listen, as gods.

Perhaps it is the act of prayer that listens
to a larger nature where the word

dissolves as food and listeners do.
Confess. Is understanding possible

when you ask a father or god in words
where does a spirit go. The word is not bread.

Not merely the body of a man or god
or both. Otherwise we would not say so.

27.

These nights I curl my body in a book.
Lips move and beg the question: who

gave us lungs in the shape of wings
that do not fly, why look up at the sky

knowing it as silent. What are words
if not gifts, in whose empty packages

we hear the voices who left us, talking.
This much is certain: we are never as

abandoned as our days and never there.
Never metaphored over the past horizon

in stories that vanish and so can never end.
My dreams are one dream now. My story

every morning made of questions. Call it
the will of dream. The paraclete, the person.

28.

My bedside table returns me to the faces,
the frames. Meet the particular mother

before her suffering made her stranger.
I hurt, I hurt, and I say I am sorry still.

The way she did once. The mere form
of sorry knelt to the height of a child.

What I say when I am not talking
is *Yes, I hear you.* I am not quite me

when I get tired and say the stupid things
in there. Somewhere. I am not you either.

Every question I ask my bedside begs
another. Can you talk with God without

your mother in the room. Or (as you close
the door) in the breath that says, *I'm sorry.*

29.

This woman whose faith suffered the fate
of millions in the ovens, she had a laugh

full of nervous decorum, a memory
for Yarhzeits, birthdays, gifts. *Can I get you*

something, she would say over and over
like a broken doll. It was annoying.

Her love, our daily bread. I cannot talk
to God without talking to her these days.

And to those inside her: the factories
that cried smoke along the clocklike railroads

of the Rhine. They know: a god alone
is never lonely. Not that far away.

Nor, I trust, as vulnerable to distance.
Not as the living are. Or the dead.

30.

You cannot love those you do not know,
a stranger told me. There is no love for love

in the eyes of animals and gardens,
however much you like the look of them.

The ache of farewell tells you something
about the choices you make like beds

for others to lie in. And you follow.
At every bedside: a clock. It watches.

It oversees the ache of memory, leaving.
Sometimes when I sleep I make the moan

fog makes when a cruiser cuts it. Coming
or going, I cannot tell. Pleasure or pain.

How oddly singular the others. How brief
this warmth across the sheets with no one there.

31.

The summons to all is not the invitation
of each. It is the head whose ear-buds

raise a song above the conversation.
Or the prurience of the guy crossing

boundaries, as if they were his. Alone.
Sometimes I think too hard or too little

to honor the voices I cannot understand.
Which is everyone. If I am listening.

Are we there yet. Must we be the only
lonely Marxists on a conference panel.

The only light on a buoy in some dark
novel impatient to be read. But hey,

my summons, my friendship, my friend, I
am here for you. Alone. Text me. Call.

32.

What this party could use is a good joke,
followed by some un-ironic weeping.

It could use a campfire outside Atlanta,
a steel cup steaming at the soldier's lip.

The past has no place to go now, and so
we go there, stone's throw from the medic's tent.

The body of the amputee will tell you,
words are not absence. I'll show you absence.

I'll show you real. I'll show you a soul
that tears away from the bone it suffers.

Real wind off the coast of the Atlantic
that comes and goes, and still I feel it.

Still the nations as they cross the river.
The men, in rivers, who lose the power of speech.

33.

And then my cat turned to me and said,
If things are only things, it is because

our relation with them is established
as understanding, in terms of a totality

that gives them meaning. I love that cat
but wondered if her eyes were too cute,

too large like those of sentimental children
come to eat the heart and all that's in it.

The immediate, she added, *cannot be*
an object of understanding. And I could not

tell if what she wanted was understanding.
Meow, she said. Was it food she wanted,

or the shuttle of talk, the back and forth
of animal angst that could have been my own.

34.

Make no mistake. I do not trust those
who love cats more than people. Or worse,

those who would ribbon them, dress them up.
What fun is pretending if it succeeds

too well. The cry out there understands
less and less the more I read there. A comfort.

To think a cat feels nothing for the fruits
and chemicals others take for food.

But who am I to say, the sentimentalist
of a skeptical nature. Long ago

I thought this love was impossible
without empathy. But that was me.

My cat is another story. *The plural of I
is not we,* she says. Or something like that.

35.

And I came to a kitchen at the end
of the world, to the foul odor that says

people sacrifice a lot for the animal.
I called my creature good because

she was not listening. I call her kind
because her needs would feed us, make us

open a thousand cans that smell disgusting.
But we were children once. Without a thought

to ask our parents how their day was.
The invention of kindness was slow, unkind.

The deferential behavior of our pets
a thing that came on us in time, pretending.

Imagine first a life without a beast.
Or a parent who did not feed you, pet you.

36.

When a cat dies, you grieve naturally.
You wait. You buy another. Your photos

shift position on the crowded mantle.
You see things in a patch of sunlight

you know are dreams and so believed.
Loneliness is just that strong sometimes.

If your personal monsters touch you
with soft coats and superstitious behaviors,

it speaks to something too specific and vague
for words. You the god grown mysterious

to these affinities with whom you sleep,
wake, and wake a little more. Always

the promise of a greater light, the dwarf
thunder of calm that shivers in your arms.

37.

Loneliness is just that political.
Here a beast on the ping pong table,

there the face of a small foreclosure.
Behind it a teller, a bank, a bank's bank.

The light we share is a nation we know
by the border guard who waves us through.

I pledge allegiance to the flag, I said
once to a flag. Talking in third person.

Mostly our failures work just well enough,
like politicians who get re-elected.

If you want to stay married, lighten up,
my marriage said. And it just might voice

the ache of particulars words repress.
Little governments with bigger causes.

38.

About now a cat wanders in to say,
Hey, I too feel strongly about the world.

The big stuff like hunger that never ends.
I give my cat a pat on the head

which might seem condescending but she
likes it. Philosophy is lonely, I say.

Especially the public spirited dialectics
who write themselves into obsolescence.

History is lonely too. History as time
longs for history as a story. You're history,

says the actor whose scene is soon forgotten.
I scare myself sometimes with stupid movies

full of real distortions. The stubborn stalker
who believes in progress. The cynic who does not.

39.

The silence of seeing and that of blindness.
They are not one silence. However one

hears one in another. Say this better,
and you might hear what Messiaen heard

in his Quartet for the End of Time,
his Abyss of Birds at the kilns of Görlitz.

He made the best with what instruments
he had: a cello, piano, a clarinet.

A god with whom he conversed in silence.
The beauty of time in the end is so much

smoke signatured in broad strokes. All
music the music of faith. It is not wisdom,

however dark the voices. But given choice,
what wisdom would curse the song inside it.

40.

I have a friend who is dead. He was
a theorist and gives flesh to theory still.

Still the hunger for the next clear thing
across the table at the Jupiter Cafe,

where he laughs at something he reads
in silence, and I say, what, as if invited.

This is the summer of his final days,
when reading, as he conceives it, has less

and less to do with meaning that survives.
When we read we are always alone,

he says, and never are. I give him that,
looking up, my book open before him

on the table, as is his, two bare fields,
furrowed in words that, abandoned, speak.

41.

I had a friend, silent on the subject
of his visits to the emergency clinic,

how he dried out in the anterooms
of death, putting all aside, disbelieving.

The watch battery of the human heart.
It takes a blinding nearness to read and replace.

A blinding distance. My friend told me
we are made of words, words of contracts.

And all of them broken. I say to him,
what about wine, it keeps its promise.

Granted, not the one you loved that loved you
once. Death made a promise to keep me

company. Hello friend, says the silence.
It makes no claim. And so cannot be broken.

42.

The great world hungers will eat themselves in time,
desired desires, gluttons for abuse.

What does it make of our commitment
to drive one another to the clinic,

if the clinician's hands are gloved in words
that cannot touch us. We are going to need

a kinder philosophy, more discerning
with knives. More embodied in a friend.

What language worth its salt would not hold us,
cure us, try. Or look at us trembling

a little at what it cannot be. Specific.
But hunger is its own attorney. And wine says,

I am the blood. And my words the flesh
they are not really, and still you beg for more.

43.

The ink blots of the analyst could use
a friend. That is what they tell me.

That is what my student from Pakistan
says with her face, as she wonders aloud

at the distance of people on buses, here,
in sweet sad America where smiles feel

mechanical, lost in chatter, hard to read.
And who am I to say it is not so.

Still our shared patterns of lonely study
lie outside the science that would call them

imperfect, as if sadness had no place
in the cry that includes us, where we live.

Me, I live with names that some call *real*,
others *shadow*, the world *a world out there*.

44.

Dear Reader, although I cannot see you,
if I did, I would need to imagine

the reader I become. Always a face
in random patterns of the wilderness.

And sometimes faces on faces better left
unseen. We must be needed elsewhere,

or why the pull, the constant visitations.
The wordlessness of witness, and that of blindness:

they are a lot like words, the way they see
their faces in others and so write letters

to no one address. My student is doodling stars
in a notebook. And she says, *back home*

we smile less and only if we're happy.
And then a star. A space. And then another.

45.

As a kid I took my smile from a mirror.
When I left, the mirror poured the rest

from its glass. Me, the mirror's mirror.
My TV laughed in all the wrong places

like a desperate friend. A distant aunt
took my hand and asked if I loved Jesus.

I said nothing. She said nothing. But she
was not looking at me. She looked up

at my father, who in turn said nothing.
So frail, this glass animal of the human

heart. I watched cartoons to get away.
Predators got hammered, then popped back

into shape, bedazzled, and the small bird sang.
And I loved that. How the hunter survived.

46.

If clowns are such friendly depressives
and town drunks, how funny can that be.

Ask the kid who laughs at the powerless
and counts himself among them. Dear face

beneath the face, who does he think he is.
But underneath him, I see a bird

alone in the cage of a woman's hand.
And trapped inside that, the song it sings.

And just maybe beyond all that, a boy.
Not the mask of the mask of a child.

But a real mask. Obnoxious with questions.
And under that, a window. Cold. Dark.

And maybe it is God's eye. Clear as night.
And maybe nothing. Like death. It's only nothing.

47.

Clarity bewilders me. *On the farm,*
my father said, *we put our animals down.*

*It's what farmers do. Animals are
animals, people people.* And the knives

at the family table await the flesh
that feeds a common spirit as we pray.

The better heaven is full of animals.
When my dog died, a friend called and said

sometimes it helps to think of all dogs
as one. But I never could. In fact I saw

my dog in all dogs. None of them mine.
And I spoke to them the way we speak

to one another when one of us is elsewhere.
You with your head in the clouds. Speak.

48.

Dogs know the real sparrow in the yard.
They read it in the dark. They know the scent

of blood that has no surrogate, no twin.
Last night my childhood hound lay down,

sighed with drool and exhaustion in bed,
and said, *animals are animals, people*

people, and I give up. Why are they so
frightened of the gods they learn to love.

And I said, *why are you so scared of thunder.*
When a friend dies, I fill a page with birds.

I write a letter no one will see. I come
to a field where there is no friend, no voice.

Only stones here and there I kneel to read.
My dog at my feet, sniffing my shoes.

49.

Today, as I wake, I become the book
the world leafs through, and I am elsewhere,

here, reading, watching a house on fire.
Then the house is mine, and me its child,

and my mother is standing beside me in the street
in silence, not knowing she is long gone now.

And though a faint smoke waters my eyes
in passing, though my roof shoulders the tower

of light, the visible night grown more so
on the brink of the unseen, I cannot bear

the same old burden. Or read the child's book
the same as pages blacken and ghost the air.

There is only so much room and fire
where the tower burns, and the eye plows on.

50.

The world without the mother, the house, the night
that turned briefly into day, it reads you

here, in the penciled occasion of your study.
It turns the page of your body at night

over and over, mercifully, missing something,
seeing its wounds in yours that are, it says,

not quite yours, but stolen, shared, reopened.
It reads and thus it sees you at a distance,

not far but far enough, across some stretch
of bells in mourning. Dear reader, dear mother,

dear fire in your tower where the old bronze
sings flashing through the garret, it reads you

who turn to smoke I breathe without knowing
I breathe and why, now, and whom I breathe for.

Acknowledgments

The author would like to thank the editors of the following journals in which sections of the book have appeared: *Arts and Letters, Asheville Poetry Review, Blackbird, Florida Review, Fiddlehead, Free Verse: A Journal of Contemporary Poetry and Poetics, Gettysburg Review*, and *St. Katherine's Review*.

Free Verse Editions

Edited by Jon Thompson

13 ways of happily by Emily Carr
& in Open, Marvel by Felicia Zamora
At Your Feet (A Teus Pés) by Ana Cristina César
Between the Twilight and the Sky by Jennie Neighbors
Blood Orbits by Ger Killeen
The Bodies by Christopher Sindt
The Book of Isaac by Aidan Semmens
Canticle of the Night Path by Jennifer Atkinson
Child in the Road by Cindy Savett
Condominium of the Flesh by Valerio Magrelli, trans. by
    Clarissa Botsford
Contrapuntal by Christopher Kondrich
Country Album by James Capozzi
The Curiosities by Brittany Perham
Current by Lisa Fishman
Day In, Day Out by Simon Smith
Dear Reader by Bruce Bond
Dismantling the Angel by Eric Pankey
Divination Machine by F. Daniel Rzicznek
Erros by Morgan Lucas Schuldt
Fifteen Seconds without Sorrow by Shim Bo-Seon, translated by Chung
    Eun-Gwi and Brother Anthony of Taizé
The Forever Notes by Ethel Rackin
The Flying House by Dawn-Michelle Baude
Go On by Ethel Rackin
Instances: Selected Poems by Jeongrye Choi, translated by Brenda
    Hillman, Wayne de Fremery, & Jeongrye Choi
The Magnetic Brackets by Jesús Losada, translated by Michael Smith
    & Luis Ingelmo
Man Praying by Donald Platt
A Map of Faring by Peter Riley
The Miraculous Courageous by Josh Booton
No Shape Bends the River So Long by Monica Berlin & Beth Marzoni
Overyellow, by Nicolas Pesquès, translated by Cole Swensen
Physis by Nicolas Pesquès, translated by Cole Swensen
Pilgrimage Suites by Derek Gromadzki
Pilgrimly by Siobhán Scarry

About the Author

Bruce Bond is the author of twenty books including, most recently, *Immanent Distance: Poetry and the Metaphysics of the Near at Hand* (U of MI, 2015), *Black Anthem* (Tampa Review Prize, U of Tampa, 2016), *Gold Bee* (Helen C. Smith Award, Crab Orchard Award, Southern Illinois University Press, 2016), *Sacrum* (Four Way Books, 2017), and *Blackout Starlight: New and Selected Poems 1997-2015* (E. Phillabaum Award, LSU, 2017). Four books are forthcoming. Presently he is a Regents Professor of English at University of North Texas.

Photograph of the author by Nicki Cohen.
Used by permission.